S0-AAD-763

Sierra Vista Middle School
Sunnyside School District 201
Sunnyside, WA 98944

THE CHANGING FACE OF
IRELAND

Text by KAY BARNHAM
Photographs by CHRIS FAIRCLOUGH

Raintree

Chicago, Illinois

© Copyright 2004 Raintree

Published by Raintree, a division of Reed Elsevier, Inc.
Chicago, Illinois
Customer Service 888-363-4266
Visit our website at www.raintreelibrary.com

All rights reserved. No part of this book may be reproduced or utilized in any form or by any means, electronic or mechanical, including photocopying, recording, or by any information storage and retrieval system, without permission in writing from the Publishers. Inquiries should be addressed to:

Copyright Permissions
Raintree
100 N. LaSalle
Suite 1200
Chicago, IL 60602

Library of Congress Cataloging-in-Publication Data:

Barnham, Kay.
  Ireland / Kay Barnham.
     p. cm. -- (The changing face of--)
  Summary: Presents the natural environment and resources, people and culture, and business and economy of Ireland, focusing on development and change in recent years.
  Includes bibliographical references and index.
  ISBN 0-7398-6044-5 (lib. bdg.)
  1. Ireland--Juvenile literature. [1. Ireland.] I. Title. II. Series.
DA906.B37 2004
941.5--dc21
                              2003000282

Printed in Hong Kong

1 2 3 4 5 6 7 8 9 0
LB 07 06 05 04 03

The website addresses (URLs) included in this book were valid at the time of going to press. However, because of the nature of the Internet, it is possible that some addresses may have changed, or sites may have changed or closed down since publication. While the author and Publisher regret any inconvenience this may cause readers, no responsibility for any such changes can be accepted by the author, the packager, or the Publisher.

Acknowledgments
The publishers would like to thank the following for their contributions to this book: Rob Bowden—statistics research; Peter Bull—map illustration; Nick Hawken—statistics panel illustrations. All photographs are by Chris Fairclough except: pp.6, 7, 28, 34, 41 Popperfoto; p.11 photo of Evelyn Cusack RTÉ; pp.16, 29 Eye Ubiquitous; pp.24, 30; 16, 29 Corbis; p.36; p.44 Camera Press Impact.

Contents

1 Cork: Past, Present and Future

Ireland is divided into four main areas: Leinster, Munster, Connaught, and Ulster, which are further divided into 32 counties. Of these counties, 26 form the Republic of Ireland and the remaining six counties form Northern Ireland, which is part of the United Kingdom. The Republic of Ireland is usually referred to as "Ireland." Its capital is Dublin.

Cork is Ireland's second-largest city. It was founded in the 600s, and since then has played a major role in the country's eventful history. The city saw bloody fighting during the Viking, Norman, and English invasions; 2.5 million people emigrated from the nearby port of Cobh during and after the potato famine of the 1840s; and violence erupted again during the Anglo-Irish and civil wars in the early 20th century.

▲ *Cork has a mixture of older buildings and new housing developments.*

Changes in Cork

Today, the many changes taking place throughout Ireland are reflected in Cork. Its population is growing every year, fueled by a high birth rate, the return of Irish citizens to Ireland, and the arrival of immigrants from other countries.

Improvements to the country's transportation network are also ongoing. In 2001, 1.8 million passengers used Cork International Airport. A new highway currently under construction between Cork and Dublin will improve travel even further. Cork is meeting the challenge of modern life while retaining its own unique, vibrant, friendly character.

▶ *The English Market in Cork is packed with fresh produce. It's also a good place to meet friends.*

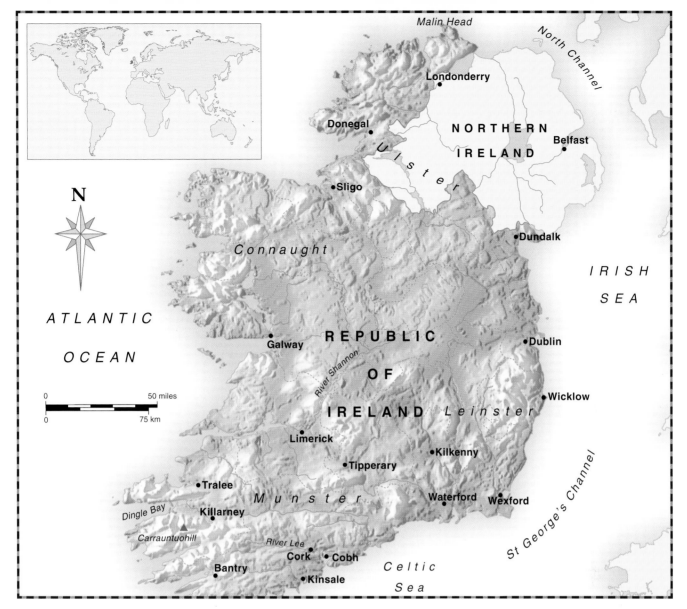

▲ *This map shows the main geographical features of Ireland, as well as most places mentioned in this book.*

IRELAND: KEY FACTS

Area: 43,671 square mi (70,282 square km)

Population: 3,883,159 (July 2002 estimate)

Population density: 89 people per square mi (54 people per square km)

Capital city: Dublin (population 953,000)

Other main cities: Cork (180,000); Limerick (79,000); Galway (57,000); Waterford (44,000)

Highest mountain: Carrantuohill (3,415 ft [1,041 m])

Longest river: Shannon (240 mi [386 km])

Main Languages: English, Irish (Gaelic)

Main religions: Roman Catholic (91.6 percent); Church of Ireland (Anglican) (2.5 percent); Presbyterian (3.75 percent); Methodist (1.5 percent)

Currency: Euro (1 euro = 100 cents)

2 Past Times

For hundreds of years, people have come to Ireland's shores eager to settle or even to rule the island. From the 1600s until the early 20th century, the country was officially a British colony. Countless Irish rebellions led to the Anglo-Irish War (1916–1921). After being defeated, the British eventually proposed that Ireland should be divided into two parts, with one small part (6 counties) remaining a part of the United Kingdom, and the majority of the island (26 counties) given complete freedom from British rule. This controversial decision, known as partition, sparked a bloody civil war, where factions fought over whether to accept the British plan or to try and unite all 32 counties.

The Irish Free State

Those who agreed with the idea of partition gained the upper hand and, in 1921, the Irish Free State was born. In 1949 it became the Republic of Ireland, with its own constitution. But the underlying disagreements about British rule were never really solved, as the continuing violence and unrest in Northern Ireland show. However, the 1998 Good Friday Agreement (also known as the Belfast Agreement) has been a major development in the peace process that will hopefully bring an end to unrest in Northern Ireland.

▲ *The Celtic cross is a symbol that dates back to the Celts, early inhabitants of Ireland.*

▼ *British Prime Minister Tony Blair and Irish Taoiseach Bertie Ahern sign the Good Friday Agreement in April 1998.*

The EEC and EU

In 1973 Ireland joined the European Economic Community (EEC), a group of countries that decided to join their economies. Now called the European Union (EU), these countries share a currency and allow free access to citizens of other EU countries. The EU also regulates trade, economic policy, and agriculture across much of Europe.

◀ *Bertie Ahern supported the "Yes" vote in the Nice Treaty referendum. Irish people were asked to decide whether or not to agree to the expansion of the EU.*

IN THEIR OWN WORDS

My name is Noreen Collins, and I'm proud to be Irish. When I travel overseas, I like to wear something white, gold, and green, to show where I'm from. Ireland has changed since I was young. For the last four generations, our land was used for farming, but now there's no money in it for small farms. People used to be self-sufficient and now they just eat fast food. It's as if supermarkets are taking over our lives. And no new houses had been built around here for over a hundred years—now they're springing up like daffodils all over the country.

3

Landscape and Climate

Ireland is the most northwesterly country in Europe. It is bordered by Northern Ireland and separated from Scotland, England, and Wales by the Irish Sea.

Coasts

Ireland's coast is 1,970 mi (3,172 km) long and is very diverse. The east and southeast coasts sweep gently into the sea, while the west and southwest coasts feature rugged peninsulas, sheer cliffs, and wide beaches, with remote islands scattered offshore.

The west coast has seen many historic moments. In 1588 ships from the Spanish Armada were wrecked here. In 1856 a transatlantic cable was laid from County Kerry to Newfoundland, Canada. Two years later, the cable was used to transmit the first transatlantic telegram, from Queen Victoria of England to President Buchanan in the United States.

▲ *Ireland has many beautiful beaches with crystal-clear water.*

Hills and mountains

Ireland's hills and mountains are relatively small—the highest, Carrantuohill, is just over a 3,000 ft (1,000 m) high. They are found mainly around the edges of the island, with the higher mountain ranges located in the west. Washed clean by the weather, the bare limestone hills of the Burren region are low, but they are very dramatic.

▼ *Most of the mountain ranges are found near Ireland's coasts. Trees have been planted along their slopes and in the valleys.*

Lowlands

The central part of the country is low-lying and wet. Most of the country's lakes, or *loughs*, are here, as are most of the bogs and marshes. Bogs are areas of wetland with acidic, peaty soil.

▼ *The lowlands in central Ireland are where much of the country's peat is found.*

IN THEIR OWN WORDS

My name is Donal Kearney and I've worked as a forester for 25 years. Forests are found in all parts of Ireland, usually on land that isn't good enough for crops. During that time I've seen lots of changes in the business. We used to use horses to cart away the timber, but now modern machinery makes the whole job much easier. The weather is wetter than it used to be, but it doesn't really affect forestry. Sitting on my machine, high up a mountainside on a bright spring day, watching the lambs and the wildlife, makes this the best job in the world.

The Emerald Isle

The Gulf Stream and southwesterly winds that blow from the Atlantic control the weather. Ireland does not suffer from extremes of temperature—it does not usually rise much above 68 °F (20 °C) or fall far below freezing.

Nicknamed the "Emerald Isle" because of its vivid green landscape, Ireland can be a very wet place to live. The most rain falls in the northwest, west, and southwest of the country, especially over higher ground. In 2000, for example, 70 in (1,786 mm) of rain fell in Kerry in the west, compared to 33 in (840 mm) in Dublin, on the east coast.

However, it does not rain all the time. Southwesterly winds mean that the weather can be very changeable; it is not uncommon to experience several sunny spells and rain showers in one day. The southeast is the sunniest place in Ireland. In 2000, Wexford enjoyed an average of 4.7 hours of sunshine a day, compared to just 3.7 in Kerry.

▲ On rainy days, the mountaintops are often hidden by clouds.

◄ Ireland rarely gets very heavy rain, but it is often drizzly.

IN THEIR OWN WORDS

My name is Evelyn Cusack and I'm a meteorologist for RTÉ—one of Ireland's television channels. Ireland is the first port of call for many of the weather systems that move across the North Atlantic. We rarely get torrential downpours or thunderstorms, but we do get a lot of "soft days," when the weather is mild and misty with light drizzle. During the last few winters, we've had very little frost, and the weather has become cloudier. However, it's difficult to say whether these weather conditions are part of natural climate change or a result of global warming.

Climate change

Since the early 1900s, Ireland's climate has become gradually warmer. Data recorded at Malin Head in County Donegal show that between 1910 and 2000 the temperature rose by about 2 °F (1 °C). Rainfall figures seem to show that the climate is getting wetter, but it remains to be seen how this will affect an island that is famous for its rain.

▼ *Despite its reputation for rain, Ireland can be a very sunny place, too!*

4

Natural Resources

Fossil fuels (including coal, gas, and peat) provide 94 percent of Ireland's electricity. However, the government is trying to reduce dependency on coal and peat, increase the use of oil, and double the use of natural gas and renewable energy by 2010.

Renewable energy

Ireland is a leading producer of wind energy, especially along its west coast. It is hoped that this and other forms of renewable energy, such as wave power and hydroelectric power, will become more common. Today, only 2 percent of Ireland's energy needs are met with renewable energy.

Bogs

Peat bogs form in very wet places and consist of layer upon layer of the partly decayed remains of dead trees and plants. Over 15 percent of the total area of Ireland is made up of bogs. Large quantities of peat are dug for domestic and industrial fuel and it provides about 10 percent of Ireland's electricity, but action is being taken to ensure that peat is conserved in the future. This is because bogs are home to many rare and protected species of plants and animals. They are also an important part of Ireland's history and scenery.

▲ *These blocks of peat have been laid out to dry.*

▼ *Peat bogs provide employment in many poor areas of Ireland. The efforts to reduce use of peat could cause unemployment.*

IN THEIR OWN WORDS

My name's David Lewis and I work in a quarry in Kilkenny. The quarry employs 70 people. We quarry limestone, which is used for a great variety of things, such as buildings, gravestones, and monuments. Our stone is also used for streetscape work—paving and guttering. We sell within Ireland, but we also export a lot of stone to Belgium, the Netherlands, Germany, and the United States. Within Europe, it helps to use the euro because we know what we're working with—there aren't any currency fluctuations to worry about, so the price of our product doesn't change from day to day.

Minerals

Discoveries of new mineral deposits in the last century have boosted the country's mining industry. In 1999, mineral output included 245,811 tons (223,000 metric tons) of zinc (the biggest deposit is at Navan, County Meath), and 43,00 tons (39,000 metric tons) of lead. Ireland is one of the leading exporters of these minerals in Europe. Slate, limestone, sandstone, and quartzite are also quarried.

◀ *Explosives are used to blast away material and quarry deep into the ground.*

Agriculture

About 20 percent of Irish land is used for farming and much of the rest is used for pasture. The best farmland is in the east and southeast, where the weather is milder. Raising cattle earns farmers the most money, followed by poultry production. The main crops are wheat, barley, oats, beets, and potatoes.

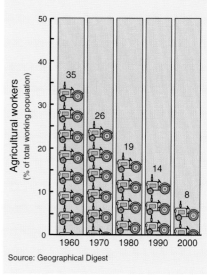

Source: Geographical Digest

▲ *This graph shows that the number of Irish agricultural workers has fallen dramatically since 1960.*

◄ *Livestock is one of the most profitable type of farming.*

When the Irish Free State was formed, Ireland was cut off from the manufacturing industry around Belfast (the capital of Northern Ireland), so, agriculture became by far the most important and successful contributor to the country's economy. Most of the farms were, and still are, small and family-run.

▼ *On a small family farm, the farmer can often barely afford to buy much machinery.*

The European Union

When Ireland joined the EEC, European prices for produce were controlled. This meant that farmers received a good price for their meat and dairy products, because the EEC promised to buy leftover goods to ensure that prices stayed high. If there is too much of one product on the market, prices come down.

◄ *It takes more machinery to look after a bigger farm.*

This system has now changed, and the EU (formerly the EEC) is encouraging farmers to rear or grow more profitable products. Farmers may now have to choose to grow other crops, or they may decide to sell their land to owners of bigger farms who have the machinery to run a farm more cheaply and so make more money.

IN THEIR OWN WORDS

My name is Paddy Murphy and I'm a strawberry farmer in Wexford. This used to be a dairy farm, but now strawberries are more profitable. I grow strawberries in plastic tunnels so that I have more control over the amount of warmth and water they get, and I don't use herbicides or insecticides. All of my produce is sold within Ireland, most of it to large supermarkets. I employ workers from overseas during the busy months of the year, but I can manage this place on my own most of the time, since almost all of the watering and fertilizing is done automatically.

5

The Changing Environment

About 35 percent of the country's population lives in Dublin. Another 7 percent lives in Cork. Over half of the population lives less than 6 mi (10 km) from the coast, which puts a strain on the roads and public services in those areas.

Housing

The population of Ireland's cities is rising. As a result, there is a need for affordable housing. Old cottages are common in rural areas, but the majority of housing is new. The number of new houses more than doubled between 1992 and 2000. Developers are now being urged to make more use of old urban areas, rather than building on more of the country's rural areas.

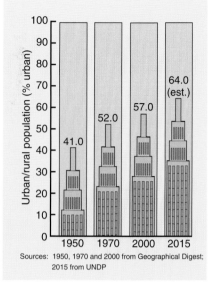

Sources: 1950, 1970 and 2000 from Geographical Digest; 2015 from UNDP

▼ *A few houses are still being built in rural areas, but this is becoming less common.*

▲ *This graph shows that almost two-thirds of Irish people will live in towns and cities by 2015.*

Rural environmental issues

Ireland is a place where trees grow easily and it is estimated that, centuries ago, two-thirds of the country was covered in forests, which have decayed to become today's bogs. But by 1900, thousands of trees had been cut down to make way for fields. At this time, 1 percent of the country was still forested. Drastic action was needed and a program to reintroduce forests began. In 1999, tree cover had risen to 9 percent and the figure is still rising. The Irish government is committed to increasing the area covered by forests in order to promote the environment, tourism, and forest-based industry.

▲ *Forestry is becoming a more important industry, and new trees are being planted all the time. Logging is carefully controlled.*

IN THEIR OWN WORDS

My name is Andrew Woodward and I'm project-managing the construction of a new section of highway between Cork and Dublin. In general, the roads in Ireland aren't that bad, although some do need maintenance. Our job is part of a strategic plan by the Irish government to improve communication routes between major cities. We have to comply with EU rules about keeping pollution to a minimum and, before work began, archaeologists came on site to search for evidence of historical settlements. We haven't faced much opposition because local people see the new road as a benefit to the community and to Ireland.

The environment

Ireland's population is expected to rise to over 4 million by 2011, increasing pressure on the country's resources and the environment. The country's main challenges are to improve the treatment of waste water, reduce solid waste, and cut greenhouse-gas emissions.

Air pollution

It is hoped that the problem of greenhouse-gas emissions can be reduced by using natural gas, rather than coal or peat, to run power stations. If Ireland reaches its proposed target of increasing tree cover from 9 percent to 17 percent of the country, then this will also help to tackle the problem. Trees absorb carbon dioxide, which is a major greenhouse gas.

During the 1990s, action was taken to deal with the problem of air pollution caused by smoky coal. Smokeless zones were introduced in heavily populated areas, where the sale and use of bituminous coal was banned. The project was considered a success and the smokeless zones are still being extended.

▶ *Peat briquets produce far less smoke than some types of coal.*

IN THEIR OWN WORDS

My name is Naomi Daly and I'm from Kerry. Nearly 4 million people live in Ireland so a lot of rubbish [garbage] is generated. Some things help to improve this situation: these "bags for life" can be recycled. A big issue in the news at the moment is whether it's better to incinerate rubbish or to dump it. Smog is a problem in big cities like Dublin and Cork, but it's improving, and the air is cleaner in the rural areas. The government should be stricter with big companies who pollute—they don't get fined enough right now.

Water pollution

Agricultural pollution, especially phosphorus output, is one of the main contributors to water pollution in Ireland, causing great harm to wildlife and the environment. Stricter environmental controls have been introduced to decrease this risk. Meanwhile, new projects are improving waste-water treatment. In 2003 Cork's new sewer network and water treatment plant were completed to deal effectively with the 15.8 million gallons (60 million liters) of raw sewage and polluted water that once flowed into the Lee River every day.

▼ *Water treatment plants are improving the quality of Ireland's water.*

Recycling

Recycling is becoming more common in Ireland, but it has a long way to go before it reaches the standard of other European countries. Most Irish people are eager to improve their environment; the main problem seems to be that they do not have enough information about the ways that this can be achieved, and they don't have the right facilities for recycling.

Dealing with waste

The Irish government is considering many different ways of reducing waste and increasing recycling. An important step will be to boost the numbers of "bring sites," where people bring glass and other materials to be recycled.

▼ *This man is helping the environment by recycling his newspapers.*

As far as glass is concerned, it has been suggested that Ireland follow Denmark's lead. Denmark reuses a colossal 496,000 tons (450,000 metric tons) of glass waste every year. Danes are encouraged to return glass bottles after use, so that they can be refilled and used again. This cuts down on the number of plastic bottles used and promotes reuse, which is much better for the environment than recycling.

Bags for life

In 2002 the government made a positive step toward reducing plastic waste. They introduced an environment tax on plastic shopping bags and encouraged shoppers to buy and reuse heavy plastic shopping bags, which are later recycled. The project has been very successful.

▶ *There are not enough "bring sites" to cope with the demand.*

IN THEIR OWN WORDS

My name is Flor McCarthy and I live in Kinsale. My wife and I have four children, so our family produces a lot of rubbish [garbage]! We've been recycling for eight years, but it's not been easy, as there are only three recycling facilities in Cork, although we've been promised another fifteen. Most waste still goes to landfill sites. A lot of rubbish is incinerated, but many people are against this because it pollutes the air. In addition to recycling bottles, cardboard, paper, and plastics, we also recycle building materials. Our house is built with lots of used bricks, timber, and doors.

6

The Changing Population

When compared to the United States and many European countries, Ireland is very sparsely populated. However, the population is concentrated in smaller areas.

A youthful country

Census information shows that the population of Ireland is getting older (the average age in 1996 was 33.6, compared with 30.8 in 1981) and that fewer children are being born. However, the country still has the highest birthrate and the youngest population in Europe.

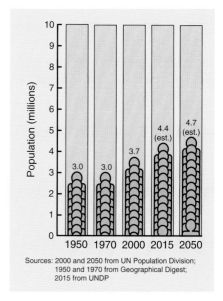

Sources: 2000 and 2050 from UN Population Division; 1950 and 1970 from Geographical Digest; 2015 from UNDP

▲ This graph shows that the Irish population is predicted to continue growing steadily.

◀ Over 40 percent of the Irish population is under the age of 25.

Life expectancy

In 1926 the average life expectancy was 57.4 years for men and 57.9 years for women. By 1996 this had risen to 73 years for men. Women can expect to live until they are 78.7 years old. These increases are linked to improved diet and health care. However, smoking is still a cause for concern. It is estimated that a third of the Irish population smoke, causing 20 percent of all deaths every year.

The Irish health service provides free health care for people on low incomes and for their families. Financial assistance is available for other people, depending on how much they earn. Alternative medicine, such as homeopathy, aromatherapy, and acupuncture, is now becoming more widely available.

◄ *Life expectancy increased dramatically during the 20th century, but women still live longer than men.*

IN THEIR OWN WORDS

My name is Mairead Hartnett and I live in Dublin. My mother married late for her generation, at 32, but my gran was married at 17. I would like to get married, but I need to meet the right guy first! I'd like to have four children. Although people are having fewer children, many Irish families are still quite large. As regards marriage, the general attitude now is that people live together for awhile first. Also, there's a new freedom to travel. People used to marry partners within bicycling distance, now we can choose from the whole world!

The Famine and emigration

In 1845, 8.5 million people lived in Ireland. The population was dependent on the potato, which was cheap to produce. Other products were grown in Ireland and exported to England, leaving no money in the hands of most Irish people. When a disease called potato blight attacked the land, people were left with no potatoes to eat and no money to buy other food. The potato crops continued to fail over the next three years, and the British government was slow in responding to the problem. By 1851, 1 million people had died from hunger and disease, and 1 million more had emigrated.

After the famine, millions more Irish people went abroad in search of work, using their earnings to support the families they left behind. The population continued to dwindle. For most of the last century, fewer than 3 million people lived in Ireland, with many young people emigrating once they were old enough to do so.

◀ *This statue in Cobh commemorates the large number of Irish people who emigrated in the 1840s–1860s.*

Immigration

However, the population has been rising steadily since the 1970s. Employment and economic prospects have improved, luring back Irish people and encouraging those of other nationalities to live there. In 1996, 7 percent of those living in Ireland were born

IN THEIR OWN WORDS

My name is Catherine Buchanan and I'm from Vancouver, Canada. I've been living in Ireland for eighteen months. I moved here with my husband, who is a civil engineer working for a construction company. I work in a lawyer's office now, but I found it difficult to get a job to begin with because it took ten weeks for my work permit to be approved. This put a lot of potential employers off. Ireland is a fantastic place to live—the pace of life is very relaxed and everyone is very friendly. However, I do miss the hustle and bustle of Vancouver.

elsewhere. Four hundred thousand Irish citizens now living in Ireland have lived abroad at some time.

But for many there is no place like home. In 1996, three-quarters of Irish people still lived in the county in which they were born.

▶ *As work prospects have improved, thousands of Irish people have moved back to Ireland to live and work.*

7

Changes at Home

Irish families have changed considerably since the 1800s. After the potato famine (1845–1849), people usually only got married if they could afford to support a family. The 1926 census shows that 84 percent of male farm laborers aged 45–54 had never married, compared to only 21 percent of farm owners.

◀ Today, many people living in Ireland were born elsewhere.

▼ Men are now more involved with child care.

Religious beliefs prohibited any form of birth control, and in 1911 the average family included 6.5 children. However, this had little effect on the size of the country's population because emigration figures were also high. By 1981, when marriage had become as popular as it was before the famine, more relaxed attitudes toward birth control meant that the average number of children per family was 2.2. In 1996 the figure averaged just 1.18 children.

Family structure

The traditional family structure is changing, too. The number of single-parent families has grown and cohabiting couples make up almost 4 percent of family units. Although divorce only became legal in 1995, the number of divorces more than doubled between 1986 and 1996.

Irish women are having children later in life, or not having children at all. The average age of all mothers in 1980 was 28.8 years, rising to 30.2 years in 2000. In 1996, 28 percent of all couples in the 25–34 age group had no children, compared with 16 percent in 1986.

▶ *The average age of women having their first child rose by 1.4 years between 1980 and 2000.*

IN THEIR OWN WORDS

My name is Kay O'Brien and I'm from Clare. Lots of things have changed in Ireland during my lifetime. Thirty years ago, the Irish were all trying to leave the country; my eldest son moved to Australia. Now, the Aussies are coming to live here! I'm happy with my life— it's easier than my mother's. In fact, nowadays, life is easier for most women. We don't have to get up early and go to the bog to dig the turf, as my mother used to do. As for my daughters, I don't mind where they live, or with whom, just as long as they're happy.

The Roman Catholic Church

On the whole, the Irish population is religious and overwhelmingly Roman Catholic (91.5 percent). The size of congregations has fallen, but many people still attend church once a week, especially in rural areas. Over twenty other denominations make up the remaining 8.5 percent of the population, and of these, members of the Church of Ireland (Anglicans), Protestants, Presbyterians, Methodists, Muslims, and Jehovah's Witnesses are the largest groups.

Pilgrimages

The most devout Roman Catholics show their faith by taking part in religious pilgrimages. These include an annual pilgrimage to the summit of Croagh Patrick—a holy mountain in County Mayo, where it is said that Saint Patrick once fasted for 40 days. Many people make the 2,500-foot (765-meter) climb in bare feet.

Each year, thousands of Roman Catholics visit a small holy island in the center of Lough Derg, a lake in County Donegal. Pilgrims show their faith by taking part in an extremely tough pilgrimage, which involves spending three days fasting, walking, and praying—all barefoot.

▲ *Simple Roman Catholic shrines are dotted around the countryside. Like this one, many are dedicated to the Virgin Mary.*

◀ *Barefoot pilgrims climb up Croagh Patrick. Every July 25,000 people make the pilgrimage.*

IN THEIR OWN WORDS

My name is Jonathan Buckley and I live in Kinsale. I'm Roman Catholic and I go to Mass every Sunday. When I'm older, I think I'll still go. More people go to church in the country than in cities. There's a very tense atmosphere in church—I'd prefer it if services were conducted in a more relaxed way, with up-to-date music and singing. Also, there should be more women preachers and priests. I think male priests are too secluded to know much about real life. Although we study religion at school, my friends and I never discuss religion outside the classroom.

The patron saint of Ireland

St. Patrick's Day is celebrated on March 17th. Many people enjoy watching or taking part in bright, colorful, and musical parades held in towns and cities around Ireland. St. Patrick's Day is also celebrated all around the world—in places as far away as Chicago, New York, and Sydney, Australia—by the descendants of the millions who emigrated from Ireland in the past. Celebrations outside the country are often more extravagant than those actually in Ireland.

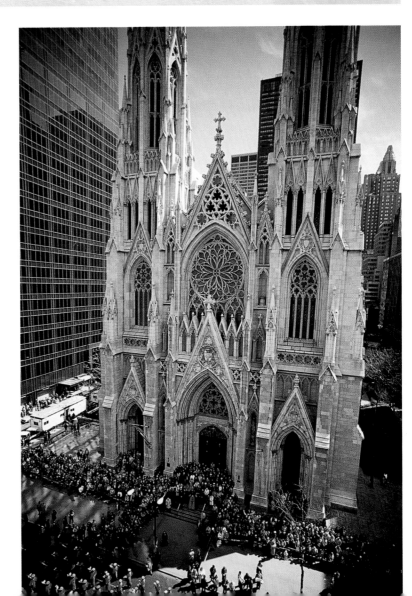

▶ *The annual St. Patrick's Day Parade passes St. Patrick's Cathedral in New York.*

Education

Irish students are staying in school longer. The number of students aged 15 and over increased by 20 percent between 1991 and 1996. The percentage of people aged 20–24 in further and higher education rose by 6 percent. These increases may be influenced by the fact that college and university education recently became free.

The Irish school system involves two main sets of exams. The Junior Cert is taken by students aged 14–15 years and covers Irish, Math, English, History, Geography, Religion, either French or German, and other subjects of the student's choice. Leaving Cert exams are taken by students aged 18–19. Irish and English are compulsory, but the students can choose their other subjects, although they must pass a total of six subjects.

▲ *A school in Ireland welcomes Mary Robinson, a former president of Ireland, to their morning assembly.*

The Irish language

Ireland has two official languages—Irish and English. Official documents, such as birth certificates and driving licenses, are printed in both Irish and English, and the names of many major public organizations are in Irish. For example, the post office is called *Oifig an Phoist.*

The Dingle Peninsula in County Kerry was one of the last places in Ireland where people spoke Irish as a first language. These areas are known as *Gaeltacht.* You still hear Irish spoken here.

▶ *In Ireland most road signs feature both Irish and English place names.*

IN THEIR OWN WORDS

My name is Margaret Kelleher and I'm a teacher in an all-boys' Roman Catholic state school in Cork city. The girls' school is next door. Lots of city schools teach boys and girls separately, although in the countryside schools are usually mixed. I teach all subjects, but Irish, English, math, and communion are regarded as being the most important. A lack of resources causes problems, as do changes to the curriculum; we need more time to retrain teachers. In the new curriculum, pupils only learn to speak Irish—they don't have to learn how to write it. This seems to be because the Irish language has no place in business in Ireland today.

Irish food

When potatoes arrived in Ireland in the 1700s, they were an expensive food enjoyed by the rich. They only became popular during the following century, when people realized how cheap and easy it was to live on them. But when the potato blight struck, so did the famine (see page 24), showing that the country couldn't rely on one type of food. However, potatoes such as Kerr's Pinks and Golden Wonder are still an important part of the Irish diet.

Many traditional Irish foods date back to before the introduction of the potato. Top Irish chefs have revived interest in these foods and cook meals using many famous Irish ingredients. These include black pudding, carrageen moss, and many types of cheese, such as Gubbeen.

The famous Oyster Festival held in Galway every September celebrates another of Ireland's traditional foods. Thousands of locally farmed oysters are eaten, and washed down with Ireland's most famous export—Guinness.

▼ *Soda bread is a traditional type of bread that is made with buttermilk.*

Healthy living

As elsewhere, supermarkets and fast-food places have made new foods available to Ireland. Dietitians worry that the population now eats too much meat and dairy products and not enough fruits, vegetables, and beans. The Irish have a reputation for heavy drinking, but this is not supported by recent evidence. Many Irish people don't drink at all.

◄ *Irish people are being encouraged to eat more fruits and vegetables to improve their health.*

IN THEIR OWN WORDS

My name is Carmel Buckley and I'm Assistant Director of Public Health for Nursing. I like to cook traditional Irish meals—I learned the recipes from my mother. My family and I keep fit. We walk or swim most days. I work as a nurse and midwife, and I advise mothers to breastfeed if possible and then to use fresh produce. Smoking is a huge problem among teenage girls. They seem to be more interested in keeping thin than worrying about their future health. I think the fashion industry is to blame: all the models seem to smoke.

Leisure time

In Ireland the pub is often the social center of a community; unlike an American bar, children are welcome and it's frequently the venue for traditional music and singing. Special occasions such as weddings would not be complete without several guests making a musical contribution.

Popular sports

In 1884 the Gaelic Athletic Association (GAA) successfully reintroduced many traditional Irish sports to the country, including Gaelic football, hurling, and camogie. These and many other sports are very popular, both with those who like to play and with those who like to watch.

▼ *Hurling is popular with players of all ages.*

Gaelic football is a mixture of rugby and football. The game is exciting and action-packed. It is interesting to note that many women both play and watch Gaelic football in Ireland.

Hurling is similar to hockey, but is played with raised sticks. It is fast, furious, and requires great skill. Hurling is becoming increasingly popular—in 2002, 84,000 people attended one match. Camogie is a gentler version of the sport usually played by women.

Soccer has become increasingly popular since Ireland first reached the World Cup Finals in 1990, and competed again in 1994 and 2002. Rugby is another favorite sport, and basketball is gaining in popularity, too.

▼ *Ireland's soccer supporters are very loyal. Here they are celebrating their 1-1 draw with Germany in the 2002 World Cup.*

IN THEIR OWN WORDS

My name is Lorna O'Brien, and I live in Donegal. Irish sports are very popular in this country. Gaelic football is played in most schools. Hurling and camogie are only played in Ireland, so counties play each other. I think it's best these sports are only played here. As for me, playing sports is very important. I try to keep fit and eat healthily so that I perform well on the running track. Last year, I competed in the All Ireland Championships—I came fourth in the 200 meter race! But it's the friends I've made through playing sports that make it so special.

Road bowling is a traditional sport now enjoyed in a few parts of Ireland. Crowds of people follow each game, the object being to throw a heavy ball as far as possible down a curved country road.

▼ *With so many miles of coastline, there is plenty of room for sailing and other water sports.*

8

Changes at Work

Ireland suffered from high unemployment for much of the 20th century. The main reason for this was that while it was a British colony, Ireland's economy was linked with Britain's. After partition in 1921, Britain's support was removed and Ireland had to develop its own economy. This resulted in high levels of unemployment, which peaked in the 1930s and in the 1980s, when almost 20 percent of men were out of work. For many people, emigration was the only way to escape unemployment.

The beginning of the 21st century has seen both unemployment and emigration fall. Between 2000 and 2002, unemployment was around 4 percent—one of the lowest figures in Ireland's history.

◀ *The opening of new computer software premises— like this Microsoft office in Dublin—led to new work opportunities in the 1990s.*

Fishing

Ireland may be a small country, but it has access to a large area of sea—13 percent of the EU's marine territory. Much of the catch is exported; of 360,000 tons (325,000 metric tons) of fish landed in 1997, almost four-fifths was sold to other countries. Just two years later, the catch had increased to 361,000. Shellfish, such as lobsters, crawfish, and shrimp, are the country's next biggest fish export.

Environmental concerns led to the Irish government banning drift-net fishing in 2002, to help prevent dolphins and other protected species from being caught in fishing nets. It remains to be seen what effect this will have on the Irish fishing industry.

▼ *The Irish fishing industry, underdeveloped in the past, is now booming.*

IN THEIR OWN WORDS

My name is Paul O'Connell and I'm a fishmonger in the English Market in Cork city. Every morning, first thing, we take two vans to Castletownbere in West Cork and buy around 50 boxes of fish. Most of our fish—sole, mackerel, flounder, whiting, haddock, and cod—is caught off the Irish coast, but other types—shark, swordfish, tuna, and turbot—are flown in daily from Europe, South America, and the United States. Ireland also exports fish to countries such as Spain, France, and Italy. One thing's for sure, there's plenty of fish in the sea around Ireland!

Irish industry

It is estimated that at least one-third of Irish industry is actually owned by foreign businesses. Many overseas companies choose to have their headquarters or large offices in Ireland, partly because the government offers tax benefits to companies that employ Irish workers. These are many industries, from manufacturers and pharmaceutical companies to technical support services.

Ireland is now the second-largest exporter of software in the world, after the United States. Many software companies have based their businesses in Ireland because of the tax benefits and also because there is an educated population available to provide the necessary workforce.

The arrival of foreign companies has brought business to Ireland and has helped to reduce unemployment, but there is a downside. There is a danger that profits made by these companies will leave the country, instead of being reinvested

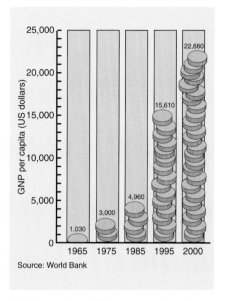

Source: World Bank

▲ Recently, GNP per capita has risen dramatically.

▼ This ship is carrying export goods overseas.

in Ireland. Also, if foreign companies go through hard times and have to reduce the size of their workforce, they may decide to close down their offices or factories in Ireland. But, for the foreseeable future, everything is going well.

▼ *Irish companies provide technical support for computer users in many other countries.*

IN THEIR OWN WORDS

My name is Brendan Kellet and I'm a training manager in a pharmaceutical company in Cork that's owned by a foreign company. I went to the University of Cork, then studied for an MA in England. I live about an hour's drive from work, but I leave early to avoid the traffic. It's worth traveling so that I can live in the country. It's a much better place to bring up children. My wife works different hours, so we hire a babysitter and, since public transportation is limited, we have two cars, so that we can both drive to work. I'd love to work four days a week, but it's unlikely it'll happen!

Women in the workplace

The number of women employed outside the home has increased considerably since the 1970s. In 1971 only 28 percent of women were employed, but by 1996, this had risen to 41 percent.

More women are returning to work after having children, and there are many reasons for this. There are now laws that aim to ensure men and women are treated equally at work, maternity leave conditions have improved, and the cost of raising a family has risen. Since April 2000 a child care program funded by the Irish government and the EU has invested millions of euros in child-care services, making it easier for more women to return to work.

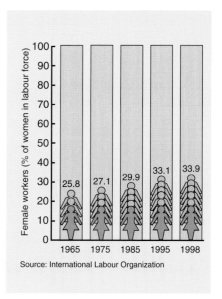

Source: International Labour Organization

▲ *This graph shows that the number of women who work has risen steadily since 1965.*

◀ *Many more women can now take advantage of the independence that having their own income brings.*

The creative industry

Ireland has a rich history of creative talent, from famous authors such as James Joyce and Roddy Doyle to pop bands including The Corrs and U2. Poets, artists, folk bands, sculptors, and the film industry have all flourished here. The Irish government is committed to ensuring that Ireland remains a popular place for artists of all kinds to live and work, so they exempt certain groups of people from paying taxes. This encourages artists to move to Ireland and gives others a very good reason to stay.

◀ *The Irish rock group U2 after winning five Grammy Awards in Los Angeles in 2002.*

IN THEIR OWN WORDS

My name is Pattigail O'Connell. I'm a florist and I started my own business in 1993. I now employ two people part-time and firmly believe that if you treat your staff well, you are repaid with plenty of hard work. I rely on my computer to receive orders from all over the world and I use it to search the Internet for information on suppliers and flowers. It isn't easy juggling work and home life, but I'm really lucky—my mother looks after my little boy two days a week. The housework does tend to suffer, though!

Tourism

More people visit Ireland than live there. In 2000, it is estimated that 6.7 million tourists visited the country. There are numerous reasons why Ireland is a popular vacation destination. Tourists come to experience the Irish way of life, the beautiful and varied scenery, the golf and fishing, and the many ancient archaeological sites. Descendants of the emigrants who left Ireland in the past often come to find out about their family's history. But, for whatever reason tourists visit, they mean big business for Ireland.

The large number of visitors in tourist "hot spots" can put a strain on local roads and services, and can lead to environmental damage. With the number of tourists rising, the tourist industry is trying to tackle this problem by promoting a variety of areas of Ireland as tourist destinations.

▲ Tourists come from all over the world to experience the Irish way of life.

◀ A tour guide tells a group of tourists all about the local sights.

Horse racing

Horse racing has been popular in Ireland for many centuries. Thoroughbreds are bred here, horses are trained here, and people enjoy going to the races here. There are estimated to be about 55,000 horses in Ireland—part of an industry that is worth millions of euros.

During 2001, both tourism and horse racing were hit by the threat of foot and mouth disease. Millions of livestock had to be slaughtered in nearby Britain, but the disease never made it to Ireland, thanks to tough rules enforced by the Irish government. Although the country lost money, this was nothing compared with the effect on agriculture if the disease had taken hold.

▼ *This racehorse is being shown at an agricultural show.*

IN THEIR OWN WORDS

My name is Teddy McNamara. I work as a tourist guide, a builder, and all-around entrepreneur! One of my favorite jobs is taking tourists round the town to show them the sights. Ireland is very popular with Americans. We're respected in the United States and Americans like to visit our country. Tourists come here from all over the world, which is great. I'm proud to be Irish, but I think that youngsters now regard themselves as being European instead. This is good for the community—it gives a broader outlook on life.

9

The Way Ahead

The last few years have seen many changes in the Irish economy. Industry has grown while unemployment has fallen, leading the media to nickname the booming economy "the Celtic Tiger." Economic growth is expected to slow down, and problems such as long-term unemployment, poverty, and the need to reduce dependency on money from the EU still have to be tackled, but the Celtic Tiger is alive and kicking. Meanwhile, as immigration figures show, Ireland is becoming an increasingly popular place to live, with a reputation for being vibrant and friendly.

▲ *Dublin, Ireland's capital city, is a major tourist destination.*

The euro (€)

On January 1, 2002, Ireland became one of the first countries to introduce the euro, the currency of the EU. The changeover was smooth, it is now easier for European tourists to spend their money, and there is a real feeling of partnership with the rest of Europe.

▶ *The modern financial center in Dublin is at the heart of Ireland's recent economic success.*

IN THEIR OWN WORDS

My name is Mark Kelleher, and I've just started studying Economics at University College Dublin. Ireland has changed a great deal over the last 20 or 30 years. When my parents were young, the nearest cinema was 80 mi (130 km) away. Now it's only 15 mi (25 km) away. There are also more airports, shops, and restaurants. The downside is that Ireland is now one of the most expensive places to live in Europe. I'm worried that prices will rise even more. However, that's in the future, so we'll just have to wait and see what happens.

A changed country

In 1845 Ireland was a country that could not afford to feed its people. Now, Ireland gives more to charity per person than any other Western European country. Irish donors give especially generously to charities helping those suffering from starvation. The country has stepped out of the shadow of Great Britain and has forged strong links with the United States and with Europe. Ireland is looking forward to an exciting and prosperous future.

▶ *Irish people give generously to charity.*

Glossary

alternative medicine medical treatment considered to be unorthodox by the medical profession

bituminous coal type of soft, black coal that burns with a very bright, smoky flame

capacity amount that something can contain

census official survey of the population, carried out at regular intervals (e.g., every ten years)

civil war war between citizens of the same country

colony country or area that is controlled by another country

constitution written principles by which a country or state is governed

currency fluctuations changes in the amounts of goods and services one country's currency will buy in another country

denomination branch of a church or a religion

economy all the activity involved in producing, buying, and selling goods, which determines how wealthy a country is. The production and distribution of a country's goods.

EEC (European Economic Community), group of countries that worked together to improve trade between member countries and later became the European Union

emigration people leaving their own country and going to live in another country

entrepreneur businessperson who starts his or her own company and is prepared to take risks and try new ideas in order to make money

European Union (EU) group of European countries that work together to achieve economic and social progress and strengthen Europe's role in the world

export product that is sold to another country

famine extreme shortage of food

fossil fuels fuels including coal, oil, and natural gas, made from the remains of plants and animals that died millions of years ago

GNP (gross national product) total value of all the goods and services a country produces in a year, including investments in the country by other nations. Per capita means per person, so GNP per capita is the total value of the goods produced, divided by the total population.

greenhouse gas gases such as carbon dioxide that are released into the air as waste products from industries and vehicles. These gases build up in the Earth's atmosphere and trap heat from the sun, leading to an increase in temperatures around the world

gulf stream warm ocean current that flows from the Gulf of Mexico toward northwest Europe

herbicides chemicals used to kill weeds

hydroelectric power electricity generated from turbines that are turned by the force of falling water

immigration people settling in a country that is not their native land

insecticides chemicals used to kill insect pests that attack crops

Irish Free State country formed from twenty-six Irish counties in 1921 and under the rule of an Irish government. It is still ruled by Great Britain.

life expectancy average length of time a person can expect to live

meteorologist person who studies the Earth's atmosphere in order to find out about and forecast the weather

partition a division. The division in 1921 of the country of Ireland into two parts, the Irish Free State (which later became the Republic of Ireland) and Northern Ireland is known as the partition.

peninsula long, thin strip of land that is surrounded on three sides by water

phosphorus chemical used in pesticides and fertilizers that causes overgrowth of water plants

pilgrimage journey made as part of a person's faith or religion

rebellion attack designed to show opposition to a government or other authority

renewable energy energy such as wind or wave power that is derived from natural forces rather than fuels such as coal that can only be burned once

smog mixture of smoke and fog

Taoiseach title of the Irish Prime Minister

trade buying and selling of things

transatlantic across the Atlantic Ocean

Further Information

Books

Cronin, Mike. *A History of Ireland.* New York: St. Martins, 2000.

Daley, Patrick. *Ireland.* Chicago: Raintree, 2002.

Minnis, Ivan. *Troubles of Northern Ireland.* Chicago: Raintree, 2003.

Useful addresses
Embassy of Ireland
2234 Massachusetts Ave NW
Washington, DC 20008
Tel.: (202) 462-3939
Fax: (202) 232-5993
www.irelandemb.org

U.S. Embassy in Ireland
42 Elgin Road
Dublin 4
Ireland
Tel.: 353-1-6688777
Fax: 353-1-6689946
www.usembassy.ie

Index

Numbers in bold are pages where there is a photograph or illustration.